Success Factors for Agile Planning

Agile Planning Successfully and Purposefully - Your Competitive Advantage

Mathias V. Waldeck

Success Factors for Agile Planning

Agile Planning Successfully and Purposefully - Your Competitive Advantage

Mathias V. Waldeck

Impressum

Bibliografische Information der Deutschen Nationalbibliothek:
Die Deutsche Nationalbibliothek verzeichnet diese Publikation in der
Deutschen Nationalbibliografie; detaillierte bibliografische Daten sind im
Internet über http://dnb.dnb.de abrufbar.

Herstellung und Verlag: BoD – Books on Demand, Norderstedt, Germany
ISBN: 978-3-7526-0211-1

Planning

The VUCA world

For some years now, articles on new and changing challenges facing the economy and people have been appearing in the press and specialist literature. Examples of this are rapid changes, the dynamics of markets and fashion trends, the ever-increasing complexity and interconnectedness of topics and systems, global competition, the speed at which markets and technologies change, and the clash of different ways of thinking, philosophies and political systems.

Many experts summarize this situation under the term "VUCA" or "VUCA world". But what does it mean to live and plan in a VUCA world and what exactly does VUCA stand for?

VUCA stands for

- Volatility (volatility)
- Uncertainty
- Complexity (complexity)
- Ambiguity (ambiguity)

Volatility (volatility)

Volatility refers to the speed of change in an industry, a market or the world in general. It is characterized by fluctuations in demand, turbulence and short time to market. We recognize increasing volatility, for example, in the speed at which technological change occurs. Due to ever more advanced technologies and the use of ever faster computers and more sophisticated development tools, we are talking in some industries about capacities and development speeds in some technologies doubling annually, for example. The more volatile the world is, the faster things change.

Uncertainty

Uncertainty refers to the extent to which we can reliably predict the future. Part of the uncertainty is perceived and associated with people's inability to understand what is going on. However, uncertainty is also a more objective characteristic of an environment. Really uncertain environments are those that do not allow for prediction, even on a statistical basis. The more uncertain the world is, the more difficult it is to predict.

Complexity

Complexity refers to the number of factors we have to consider, their diversity and the relationships between them. The more factors determine or influence a situation, the greater its diversity and the more they are interrelated, the more complex an environment is. When complexity is high, it is impossible to fully analyze the environment and reach rational conclusions. The more complex the world is, the more difficult it is to analyze. [1]

-----

[1] In this context, we would also like to refer to the Cynefin model by Dave Snowden.
Wikipedia.com

"The Cynefin framework is a knowledge management model with the task to describe problems, situations and systems. The model provides a typology of contexts that give an indication of what kind of explanations or solutions might apply.

Cynefin is a Welsh word that is usually translated in German as 'Lebensraum' or 'Platz', although this translation cannot convey its full meaning. A full translation of the word would imply that we all have several pasts of which we can only be partially aware: cultural, religious, geographical, tribal, etc.

The term was chosen by Welsh scholar Dave Snowden to illustrate the evolutionary nature of complex systems, including their inherent uncertainty. The name is a reminder that all human interactions are strongly influenced and often entirely determined by our experiences, both through the direct influence of personal experience and through collective experience such as stories or music.

The Cynefin framework is based on research from the theory of complex adaptive systems, cognitive science, anthropology and narrative patterns, and evolutionary psychology. It "explores the relationship between people,

Ambiguity

Ambiguity refers to a lack of clarity about how something is to be interpreted. For example, a situation is ambiguous if information is incomplete, contradictory or too imprecise to draw clear conclusions. More generally, ambiguity refers to vagueness and uncertainty in ideas and terminology. The more ambiguous the world is, the more difficult it is to interpret. Ambiguity often results from a different context of the observer. Different world views, educational standards, cultural backgrounds, or similar factors can lead to the same information being understood and interpreted differently by different people.

---

experience and context" and proposes new ways of communication, decision making, policy making and knowledge management in complex social environments.

(access 8/2020)

Problems of traditional planning

Living in a "VUCA world" has an impact on how we plan and how successful planning is. Traditionally, planning often takes place on the basis of some kind of specifications or requirements document. The aim is to describe and plan the state after the change or development as precisely as possible. Often the corresponding information also becomes part of an agreement or a contract, which has to be realized in the context of a project or a change process. The implementation based on this can take months or in some cases years, within which the existing plans are worked through. Projects are generally considered successful if the specified requirements are implemented within the specified cost and time frame and meet the specified quality criteria. Time and again it can be seen that in the course of the project, general conditions, markets, legislation, own company positioning, existing customer requirements or technological conditions are subject to change. In the case of short projects this is less significant, in projects with implementation periods of sometimes several years the effects of VUCA factors can be considerable.

Of course, changes are also possible within the framework of a traditionally managed project. However, this form of project in the agile area is not called "waterfall" project management by chance, because as long as the process is followed, i.e. the individual project phases are carried out as planned, a familiar stream bed can be passed through with the implementation. This means effort, but is guided through the known process. At the moment when changes

(VUCA) are not only perceived, but should also have an impact on the project, we basically have two different options:

- Continuation of the existing project as defined, knowing that further project phases must be scheduled after project completion to implement existing change requests.
- Adapt the existing project and thus leave the existing process plan.

Continuation of the existing project

In the present case, the continuation of the existing project offers the advantage that, at least in the short term, everything can continue to run as planned. Budgets, costs, time frame, personnel requirements, etc. will continue to exist at least until the end of the original project and during the corresponding period of time there is the possibility to extensively plan the follow-up project. The disadvantage is undoubtedly that funds and time are potentially used for the implementation of requirements that are not (or no longer) needed in the implemented way and that further costs and implementation times will arise for the follow-up project, which also means that the results of the project can only be benefited from later. The fact to implement things that are not needed at all will also hardly have a positive effect on the motivation and project identification of the team, which potentially leads to further costs, delays and possibly even a reduction of quality.

Adapting the existing project

The alternative is to adapt the existing project. Apart from the fact that this means that the existing process cannot continue as before and must either be completely aborted or adapted based on "ad hoc planning", an appropriate adaptation means that all previous steps must be analyzed and partly revised. This concerns the business case, the project and possibly existing phase plans, if not yet implemented, the associated risks, quality management measures, budgets for time and costs and possibly even the contracts or agreements with customers and subcontractors on which the project is based. Of course, the extent of the need for adaptation depends on the extent of the change to be implemented. Accordingly, this is also an important aspect for the selection of the appropriate approach.

Agile Planning

If we assume a VUCA world in which change is a basic pattern in various respects and for various reasons, we are dependent on a type of planning that not only accepts change with considerable effort, but also sees the handling of changes in the world as part of the model, so to speak. Agile planning - based on short development cycles and continuous review and adaptation of requirements - is a widely and successfully applied process model. What does this mean?

The first step of agile planning is to formulate a clear picture of the goal. However, this picture should not describe the implementation method, but the state after the change. What do we want to achieve? What is the world, the product, the company, the process ... after the change we are striving for. The question of how to achieve this is important. In this first step we should consciously detach ourselves from it, because otherwise we might lose sight of possible solutions too quickly and focus on one - not necessarily the optimal - path. In addition, the more we lose ourselves in details at this point in time, the more we restrict our options for action and decision-making. So let us stay open and focus on the big picture!

In an agile context, we generally call this image we are developing a "vision". Although this is sufficient in most cases, a vision can be a challenge for a team. There is a danger that even with a good description, different people will develop a different picture of the solution based on their knowledge and background. One approach that is often helpful in this context is to jointly concretize the vision in a workshop for the participants (both on the stakeholder and the implementer side). One method that I like to use is the joint, iterative development of a business model canvas on the topic. Robert C. Mir describes a sketch of a possible approach in his book "Iterative Business Model Canvas Development - From Vision to Product Backlog". The focus here is not the creation of concrete requirements, user stories or similar, but the joint development of an even stronger vision and its consideration from the different dimensions of a business model canvas. A completely different approach, but one which can serve the same purpose, is the joint creation of a solution picture within the framework of a Lego® Serious Play® Workshop.

If a common, strong and attractive vision of the future product or condition now exists, the next step will be to define first steps towards implementation. Do not fall into traditional patterns and do not try to create a kind of specification sheet. Rather, you should limit yourself to creating a few requirements, whose implementation may already offer initial customer benefits and further insights into the requirements and characteristics of the vision. Try to free yourself from the pressure that the requirements found must necessarily be the best and in any case represent the first steps of the best possible solution.

This does not mean that you should carelessly describe something banal, but only that you must be aware from the very beginning that agile product development means in any case that we try to find a solution of maximum value for the customer, but that this can also mean that after implementing a requirement we find that it does not yet meet the desired customer benefit and may have to be adapted or even replaced by another version.

It is an important insight of an agile team that agile approaches lead to development starting before a final, detailed solution picture exists - indeed, that such a picture is never available during the development process, but develops through implementation and the feedback received afterwards. The three pillars of Scrum are "transparency", "review" and "adjustment". We are in agile development in a constant learning process, in which we continuously approach the desired level of customer benefit.

For the role of the Product Owner, whose task is to maximize value for the customer and who therefore also has a responsibility for a reasonable cost-benefit ratio (of whatever kind), it is often a difficult step - which is especially difficult for less experienced Product Owners or people with a strong project management background - to start implementing requirements so early in a project and thus to enter very uncertain terrain. However, this is a natural consequence of implementing a VUCA project in a VUCA world, i.e. a project that not only endures the VUCA elements of volatility, uncertainty, complexity and ambiguity, but also understands and welcomes them as an opportunity and guideline for product development.

In a first development cycle, the first prioritized requirements (Product Backlog Items) are now addressed. The selection of the requirements will be done by the development team taking into account existing prioritizations by the product owner. The available number of requirements is generally still small at this point in time. The earlier the team starts to implement requirements, the smaller the available worklist. Especially in this early phase it is possible that the requirements have not yet reached a "ready" status, i.e. not all questions that are necessary for implementation have been clarified and possibly not yet estimated. This may not be ideal. However, it is still worth starting early on, because during the implementation process we are able to gain further insights into the vision to be realized on the one hand, and on the other hand to get initial feedback from the stakeholders during sprints in the review.

Based on further discussions between the product owner and various stakeholders during the development cycle (Sprint) and the feedback at its end (Sprint Review), we gain further insights that enable us to create new requirements and adapt existing ones if necessary. It may also be that this makes the vision more tangible. The new findings are then used to plan the next iteration. Our vision of the solution has thus become more concrete, without being negative towards changes or new requirements. Rather, the participants experience that in the course of the work, more and more mutual knowledge for the solution and mutual understanding for the questions and challenges of the other participants grow. Agile development should always be seen as a joint effort of development (methodological and technical competence) and stakeholders (professional competence). It requires close, motivated cooperation between both areas, or, as the Agile Manifesto puts it in the Principles:

"Technical experts and developers must work together on a daily basis during the project. [2]"

Based on the additional knowledge and experience (we therefore also speak of empirical process control) the next development cycle can be tackled with Sprint Planning. In this way, we move sprint by sprint towards the realization of the vision.

---

[2] Source: https://agilemanifesto.org/iso/de/principles.html

Planning Onion

Agile planning based on vision and product backlog is sufficient to create successful products. However, this often does not meet the requirements of the various internal and external stakeholders. In order to be able to assess measures such as training, implementation, commissioning or financial burdens and risks, planning data is required that goes beyond the content of the current sprint. On the other hand, it is also necessary to have a largely day-to-day planning within the coordination of the development team or teams. This approach of planning on different levels is often compared figuratively to an onion with different enclosing shells. It is also called the "planning onion".

Basically, such a shell model can be thought of as a shell that covers the strategic planning of an organization. However, on the level of what we look at in the day-to-day business of agile development teams, the topic of product planning is probably the outermost shell, which we should look at in more detail.

Let us take a closer look at the following levels and their dependencies:

- Product Planning
- Release planning
- Sprint Planning
- Daily planning (Daily Scrum - coordination of the team)

Product Planning

Product planning is generally based on a product vision that has been developed and concretized together with the customer, which is the goal. If we move in an agile context, then product planning will not be presented in the context of concrete requirements documents but will have more the character of a directional statement. Some agile methods provide for certain project phases in their process model, which are concerned with questions such as feasibility or the development of basics[3], others such as Scrum do not define these tasks further. Methods that are often used in this planning context are creative methods such as Design Thinking, Design Sprinting, Vision Boarding, Lego® Serious Play® or a variety of methods and approaches from classic requirements engineering. The question of detailing and concretizing such approaches is always a great challenge. It is of course useful to get a picture of what needs to be achieved; however, there is always a certain tightrope walk between what is considered defined and what can be changed in the context of agile development based on the experience and knowledge gained in the VUCA world.

In interaction with release planning, product planning can also be understood to be release-based, whereby the current or next release

---

[3] Frameworks such as DSDM, where a separate feasibility and foundation phase is part of the process model, should be mentioned here - whereby DSDM is an agile method, but not a scrum-based framework.

is discussed in more detail than later releases, the scope and design of which are largely based on experience and feedback from previous releases.

Release planning

Like agile planning, agile release planning can be seen as an overall iterative process. The planning for the next release(s) will be more concrete than the planning for those that lie further in the future. It must always be agreed how agile the mentioned planning should be. If we speak of a completely agile planning, we will always have the challenge that everything that has not yet been implemented is still subject to possible adjustments. However, there is also the possibility of taking a more pragmatic approach to release planning, which is often used in the context of larger organizations or customer/supplier environments in particular, where it is assumed that the contents of releases are more or less fixed [4]and that only detailed adjustments will be made, whereas the contents of future releases may have greater or possibly even absolute degrees of freedom with regard to content, scope and characteristics.

When we talk about product planning, we have to understand that such an approach always means a certain compromise to complete agility, but in many contexts, it is in line with current conditions. In a fully agile environment, there is no actual product or release

---

[4] This does not refer to the detailed requirements, but to the larger function blocks, which are often represented in the form of epics or features

planning, but we are moving in the area of conflict between vision and iteration. Accordingly, it seems important to emphasize that a decision for agility is rarely an absolute decision of "YES - we are completely agile" or "No - we are not doing anything agile", but rather a question of choosing an appropriate level of agility that can be adapted over time as development progresses.

With regard to agile release planning and corresponding methods, there is a separate, more detailed section in the same book.

Sprint Planning / Iteration Planning

The planning of a Sprint, as an iteration in Scrum is called, is a joint effort of the product owner and the development team based on their orientations and goals. The Product Owner provides a template by prioritizing requirements in the Product Backlog to maximize the value of the resulting solution and proposing a Sprint goal. Based on this, the development team decides what should/can actually be implemented. This is usually based on considerations of capacities, possible dependencies, but also on a good workload for the team. While the actual sprint planning takes place at the beginning of the sprint in the context of a special event of the same name, the necessary preparatory work (discussing and processing requirements, clarifying questions, estimating effort, prioritizing, and, if necessary, splitting requirements into smaller, less extensive requirements [story splitting]) is done continuously. The corresponding work is performed within the activity Backlog Refinement - also called Backlog Grooming by some authors.

There is also a separate chapter in the book on the topic of iteration planning/sprint planning.

Daily Planning

In agile teams, daily planning is generally done directly by the development teams. In Scrum this is generally determined by the Daily Scrum, where each developer shows which work packages he has completed and which he will work on next. If we start out from the agile idea of self-organized and self-responsible teams, appropriate control or influence cannot come from outside the team.

Release planning

Release planning is a special challenge in the agile area. What exactly should be planned? After all - if we take the topic of agility seriously - the requirements to be implemented are not finally defined, but develop during the course of the project based on new insights, requirements and the feedback from stakeholders. An "exact" release planning is therefore hardly to be expected in an agile context. However, the idea that all requirements would change at any time and thus be virtually arbitrary is also somewhat unworldly.

If we take a closer look at product requirements, we find that very different types of requirements come together. This not only concerns the scope or content of requirements, but also their importance or added value. In order to gain an overview, it has proven to be useful to prioritize the requirements in terms of the added value for the customer (according to whichever criteria they are defined). One approach that has proven itself in various methods and originally comes from the context of the agile project management method DSDM and was later used in Prince2, for example, is MoSCoW prioritization. Here, requirements are classified into one of four categories:

- M - Must have
- S - Should have (target criterion)
- C - Could have (optional criterion)
- W - Won't have this time (not included)

It is crucial that the various categories are defined somewhat differently than we know from many requirements documents - where 99% of customer requirements are defined as "must have" criteria, which takes the whole issue of prioritization ad absurdum - because we start from very clear definitions:

Wikipedia holds a more precise definition of the four categories:

"Must

Must describes requirements that are essential for the project and are not negotiable. Failure to implement them in whole or in part would lead to the failure of the project. Requirements of this kind are summarized in the project timebox. MUST is also an acronym - Minimal Usable SubseT - and stands for Minimal Requirement.

Should

Although should requirements are not critical to the success of the project, they are highly relevant and should be considered in the project implementation, as long as no impairment of must requirements occurs. Should requirements can often be implemented in different ways.

Could

Could requirements have a low relevance and are often called Nice to have. They are only taken into account if capacities are available in addition to the priority processing of must- and should-requirements. But Could requirements should not be ignored in general. Often a few easy to implement Could requirements can generate a considerable added value with minimal, additional development costs.

Won't

Won't requirements are of lowest priority for the current project or planning phase. However, and this is one of the biggest advantages of MoSCoW, the classification as Won't shows that the requirement is professionally and/or technically important, but not time-critical. Requirements classified in this way are not forgotten and are prioritized again for the planning of the next release.

A good wordlist produces three decisive effects:

1. No stakeholder has to "fight" for the acceptance of requirements
2. When considering future requirements, current ones are also reconsidered
3. When the designers see the long-term planning, they can already make provisions for later implementation during the current realization

The advantages of the MoSCoW prioritization method are that, in contrast to simple numerical 1-3 prioritization, it can be clearly and comprehensibly defined which requirements are time-critical and *have the greatest business impact. Both functional and non-functional requirements are taken into account.*

If this prioritization is applied correctly, we find that in the vast majority of projects, only a handful of requirements will be assigned to the "must-have" categorization, more will belong to "Should have" and even more to "Could have".

We also find that the probability of major adjustments or even the elimination of "must-have" requirements is very low. Of course, detailed adaptations may be necessary, but these are usually of marginal importance in terms of planning in terms of effort and implementation time.

This brings us to a helpful point for agile release planning. We have found a not absolute, but still relatively strong correlation between "important requirements" (requirements with a high benefit) and "stable requirements", which we can take advantage of if necessary.

When we implement requirements in an agile context, most frameworks follow the maxim that we deliver maximum value to the customer as early as possible. Unlike in a project with a "waterfall" approach, where we assume that we implement all requirements anyway, in the Scrum context our approach is that we want to implement the requirements with maximum value added as early as possible and complete the project when sufficient value has been realized.

So for agile release planning, this means that we will tend to design release planning in such a way that we strive to deliver must-have requirements early. These requirements are stable and generally subject to fewer fluctuations and changes. We will address them early and clarify them in the context of Refinement. This does not mean that requirements cannot still be changed, but as described, these changes will rarely be far-reaching.

Of course, the idea of exclusively implementing requirements of maximum added value for the customer is illusory. For the development and operation of solutions, we need not only the central elements of an application or product, but also numerous less value-adding requirements that are important for orderly and simple operation. These requirements must also be planned and, of course, not all of them can be implemented at the end of the project, because this would possibly reduce the possibility of an early release. Accordingly, a mixture is important for planning.

It can be useful to focus on the communication of the high-priority requirements and to use the less high-priority ones as filler material, so to speak, which can be postponed to a later release if necessary. On the other hand, this can ensure that the planning of the high-priority requirements, which are usually also of the highest interest to the stakeholders, can be carried out with a high degree of reliability and relatively few changes.

Content vs. Time

When we talk about release planning, it is important to understand that there is no one right way to plan releases, but that it can change according to different circumstances. On the one hand, there may be certain framework conditions for release, but on the other hand, there may be certain requirements from stakeholders in terms of planning and planning accuracy. This could be of particular importance, for example, if a project and its results have to be coordinated with the results of other projects running in parallel.

Basically, we can distinguish two basic forms of release planning - independent of "agile" or "non-agile". One is content-based, the other time-based.

Content based release planning

Content-based release planning determines which requirements are part of a release. Depending on the scope or frequency of releases, this can lead to certain difficulties with regard to agile product development. If the defined requirements are successfully implemented, the release is carried out. The release date can be earlier or later - based on the implementation speed etc.

Time-based release planning

Time-based release planning is particularly important if the release has an external, time-based dependency. This can be the case if, for example, certain fixed maintenance intervals have to be used to implement a solution, or if there are dependencies on external developments which have to be released in parallel or based on them. A pure point in time based release planning describes a release date or a release period and will release those requirements which are already realized. What is not yet or only partially completed at the respective date will not be released and will usually be included in one of the next releases.

The best of both

A combination of prioritization (e.g. MoSCoW prioritization) and time-based release planning generally allows an approach that achieves an optimal combination of requirements for agility and response to the VUCA world and the requirements of those involved in the planning.

MVP product and release planning for advanced users

A special form of product and release planning is based on the MVP approach announced by Eric Ries in his book "Lean Startup". MVP stands for Minimum Viable Product - i.e. the smallest possible partial product that is viable, or, in other words, that makes sense in the company and helps us to gain further insights. In an agile context, the approach is often used in combination with the User Story Mapping approach[5].

Wikipedia describes the MVP as follows:

"The term MVP comes from the Lean Startup idea, and was coined in 2001 by the entrepreneur Frank Robinson and popularized by Steve Blank and Eric Ries. The quickly and easily created product is equipped with only the most necessary core functions, e.g. (for an Internet-based product) by a landing page, in order to save work, money and time. It will be published to get feedback from (potential) customers; early adopters who can best understand the product's intent play a special role. The feedback is then used to expand and improve the MVP round by round.

---

[5] Patton, Jeff with Peter Economy (2014). User Story Mapping. (O'Reilly Media)

The goal of this strategy is to avoid products that customers do not want. The information gained about customer wishes should also help to steer the capital investment towards the best product".

When using the MVP approach in the context of agile product and release planning, the basic challenge is to determine a meaningful number and selection of requirements for the product to be created, which, once implemented, meet the following requirements:

- The resulting product enables a meaningful delivery to the customer - this does not mean that all conceivable or presumably desirable requirements have been implemented, but only that the implemented requirements enable applicability.
- The resulting product provides the basis for obtaining helpful feedback from the users, which gives both clues as to whether the product will be accepted in principle, and also allows insights into which further requirements will enable special added value/ special benefits for the customer.
- The resulting product meets the requirements of the Definition of Done and thus complies with the agreed quality specifications.

The requirements that we are setting out in the definition of the future MVP are those that will be implemented in the first release.

Depending on the further approach, requirements going beyond this can already be provisionally assigned to further releases (e.g. based on thematic context); however, it must be taken into account that this assignment is only provisional and - based on the experience gained during implementation and especially based on feedback from customers - in extreme cases may require a complete change.

One approach that corresponds to particularly agile thinking in this context is when the MVP is actually understood as a separate product. For this purpose, the client provides, plans and implements a budget. Once the MVP has been released - generally at a reasonable price - and we have gathered experience based on this, a lot of additional information can be gained:

- Is there interest in the product - and how much money is willing to spend on it?
- What concrete requirements do customers expect (possibly even more precisely divided into different customer segments or similar)?
- Was the technical approach basically target-oriented or are adjustments necessary?
- Are there any additional market segments which we had not considered before and which might have different requirements and a different use?
- ...

Based on the experience gained in this way, further data is obtained, which in turn may represent a business case that deviates from the original assumptions. Depending on the findings, the client can determine whether further investments are worthwhile, in which topic areas/features further investments should be made and which ones may no longer enjoy the previous prioritization, etc. In short, it is possible to finance and release projects based on individual releases and thus operate much closer to the market and customer benefit.

Sprint Planning

The next level in the planning onion is the planning of the iteration. In Scrum we speak of Sprint. It is about the development cycle in which the various activities or process steps are run through, in which usable subproducts are created from requirements, which are not only developed, but also tested and documented.

Sprint planning requires four different pieces of information, which are partially interdependent:

- What is to be achieved - This is the question of the sprint goal.
- What capacity does the team have - how much machining capacity is available during development?
- Which competencies are available and to what extent?
- What effort (and, if applicable, which competencies) is needed to implement the various requirements?

Many authors neglect in their descriptions the topic of the different competences within the team and the requirements. After all, we assume self-organized, cross-functional teams. But some, even renowned authors, such as Mike Cohn, for example, emphasize that the question of the different competencies and skills of individual team members certainly plays a role.

What should be achieved?

Many Scrum teams do not know the term "sprint goal" or think that the sprint goal is simply to implement the agreed (committed) requirements. This is not the case. The sprint goal is very important for the self-conception of what we do in Scrum (or other agile frameworks). In contrast to classical project management, where the question of what is to be implemented and achieved is mainly asked at the beginning of the project and the main task of the project is to implement what has been agreed upon within the agreed framework, the most important goal of agile development is the realization of added value (benefit) for the customer and the project has a justification as long as the resulting effort is in an attractive ratio for the customer due to the added value it creates.

The Sprint goal now describes what we will realize in terms of value creation for the customer in the next development cycle. It is thus part of the project rationale presented in the vision and is intended to focus on the customer's benefit rather than simply working through lists. This project goal is also what we mainly communicate with stakeholders; the motivation of the team (instead of working through lists to achieve something for the customer) also depends on it, and it is especially what gives the legitimacy, so to speak, for the fact that effort is generated for the realization of the sprint.

This is of such importance that the omission of this sprint goal (when it becomes "obsolete") is the only legitimation for aborting the sprint as presented in the Scrum Guide. The sprint goal also defines the requirements to be implemented (Product Backlog Items) - these are essentially those that contribute to the realization of the sprint goal. If this is not possible, for example, because too many or extensive requirements have to be realized to achieve the sprint goal, the sprint goal will have to be changed. It is the sprint goal (not the individual requirements) that the development team will finally commit to at the sprint planning meeting.

What capacity the team has

In his Nokia test, which he designed for the company of the same name as a test to determine the agile maturity level and status of the team(s), Jeff Sutherland made the question of whether the team knows its own velocity one of the central questions for determining the maturity level of Scrum teams.

This certainly does not mean that the question of whether everyone in the team can remember a certain number is a central quality feature. Rather, it is a question of whether the team is at all concerned with its capacity and accordingly attaches importance to continuously optimizing this capacity in the context of its own development (continuous improvement).

The capacity of the development team is generally determined based on past results. Most teams use Story Points and describe the velocity as the number of Story Points they realized in past sprints. Some always use the last value, some use the average of the last three or five sprints, some use the overall average, and some modify the values to remove certain outliers, for example by not counting the first few sprints. In fact, the question of how to determine the capacity of the team is of secondary importance. Two issues are important: a) It should be done in a way that allows the team to measure its own progress and set appropriate goals; and b) It should be done in a way that is understandable to all parts of the team and allows the team to identify with and work on the results. In contrast, a comparison across teams is neither goal-oriented nor meaningful.

Which competencies are available and to what extent?

This point is actually very controversial in the agile community and also in the context of Scrum. After all, we don't want to divide the development team further and it would be dangerous to determine how many people in the team are familiar with a certain technology or method. It would offer the possibility that the team would not continue to see itself as a team in which all members are equally responsible for implementing the requirements and support each other. The danger of mutating into a group of professionals where everyone does their own thing and then "goes home" seems to be in the air.

In fact, one should consider here that there will of course be people with different competencies and skills in teams and that - especially if a development depends on different competencies and skills - it is important for the question of what can be realized within a sprint whether people take over tasks within their core competencies or whether they support other team members in their core competencies.

In terms of team development and the expansion of capacity and efficiency, it makes sense for the individual team members to support each other and also to get to know each other's abilities better. Techniques such as peer programming can be of great benefit here. However, they are more effective in the context of longer-term team development. In the short term, therefore, it makes sense to also consider the question of the skills required for this when planning the work to be implemented in order to use team resources as efficiently as possible. This should not in any way lead to the team stopping supporting each other and always performing tasks as a team task, but only to finding a sensible measure that also ensures that benefits can be made available to the customer as early as possible.

The scope of the various requirements

In order to determine what is to be implemented within a development cycle, not only capacity but also the amount of work involved in each task is crucial. The question of the individual efforts that are required for different competencies can also be asked - but as mentioned, this is a controversial issue. In any case, based on the agreed upon sprint goal, the selection of the requirements to be implemented takes place by comparing available capacity with estimated effort. There are two approaches, whereby the first corresponds to the statements of the Scrum-Guide, whereas the latter is more of a pragmatic approach, which was especially described by Mike Cohn.

- Velocity-based sprint planning
- Comittment-based sprint planning

Velocity-based sprint planning

Velocity-based sprint planning is nothing special for most Scrum teams. Velocity is determined based on the productivity of previous sprints. This can be done in different ways, as already shown. Based on this, the appropriate number of Product Backlog Items is selected. The team can tend to choose rather cautiously and stay below the previous average, or it can be ambitious and thus go a bit beyond the previous performance.

In addition to the pure number of past sprints, teams often also include already known absences or other capacity reductions and reduce the available capacity accordingly.

In theory, many teams believe that the correct procedure for selection during the sprint planning meeting would be for the team to start with the request to which the product owner has assigned the highest priority in the product backlog and to carry down the product backlog items until its own capacity limit is reached. Finally, the Product Owner is responsible for prioritizing the Product Backlog and accordingly it seems as if his template is to be followed. In some teams, the Product Owner even makes firm commitments to the customer before the sprint begins, based on the prioritization, which are then implemented in the next sprint.

That is project manager thinking. In connection with planning in Scrum this is not appropriate. We rightly speak of a self-responsible development team, which as such naturally also decides what tasks it wants to implement as part of a sprint. Of course, this should not completely deviate from the Product Owner's prioritization, but it should also not create an automatism.

On the one hand, there is the question of the extent to which requirements support the sprint goal proposed by the product owner. If it turns out that the team cannot support the proposed sprint target and a different sprint target has to be defined, this may result in a completely different selection of Product Backlog Items that support the new target.

However, a self-organized, experienced team will always have its own skills and team composition in mind when choosing stories. What is feasible and sensible? Let's imagine - to illustrate an extreme case - that one team includes an expert for creating interfaces with a special development environment and programming language, but the others, at least currently, have no experience with the topic. Let's further imagine that the data transfer to the interface is extremely important, since it is the interface that makes payment transactions possible in the first place, and accordingly, at the start of sprint planning, the five highest priority requirements are those that fall precisely into this area.

Now the team could actually select all these interface items and agree on a corresponding target. However, the colleagues would know that one developer would be active in the area of his core competence, but all others would have to somehow try to implement corresponding requirements with manuals, tutorials and a lot of support from the said colleague. It goes without saying that the quality of this work would probably be much lower than if it had been done by a specialist, and that considerably more time would be needed for this.

At first glance, this corresponds to the idea of a team where everyone does everything and helps each other. But in reality this is simply a waste of capacity. Of course, it makes sense and is desirable if employees in teams start to share their knowledge with others in order to be able to work together more flexibly and in a more goal-oriented manner. But this is a process. Accordingly, it makes sense for a team to take a closer look at requirements together, always being aware of what the individual skills and competencies of the various team members are like and what meaningful choices are available. Accordingly, it may well be that there is a certain flexibility in the choice of Product Backlog Items for different reasons - the one described is just one example. It is best if the participants in the meeting have an open discussion here, which can also lead to the Product Owner gaining a better understanding of how he can sort the Product Backlog more sensibly in the course of his work.

A method that at first glance seems to be incompatible with the Scrum Guide, but is characterized by a high degree of pragmatism, is the Commitment-based Sprint Planning, as it was presented by Mike Cohn among others.

1. The team proceeds in such a way that the top story that supports the sprint goal is shared in the product backlog. In the Refinement process this story was discussed earlier and is known to all participants at least in principle.

2. The team looks at the story and sees what effort is required in terms of the various skills needed for implementation. If the whole thing is still feasible for all involved within the available capacity, everyone agrees and the Product Backlog Item is transferred to the Sprint Backlog.

3. The team moves on to the next item. The various competence representatives have in mind how much of their capacity is already occupied for the already selected task. Together, they compile a new story and determine the effort required for the various competencies. The different competence representatives check whether their respective competences are still sufficient for the realization of the story. If this is the case, the product backlog item in question is also transferred to the sprint backlog and the next story is started; if not, the next story is looked at. This means that when selecting a story, the commitment of the whole team to take over the story must always be present. If a team

member does not consider the implementation realistic, based on his capacity planning, either an alternative approach is found or the story is put on hold.
4. This is done until the various fields of competence have a suitable workload.

My practical experience is that this approach works very well and especially promotes team spirit. Although it makes less mutual support in the implementation necessary, it helps the team on the one hand to gain a better understanding of the work of the others and, as a self-organized team, on the other hand to recognize better where know-how transfer and know-how building is important for the work of the team, so that more competent mutual support is possible in the future.

Agile estimation

The estimation of product backlog items is an important prerequisite for meaningful sprint planning. Only if a comparison of capacity and effort for the individual stories is possible, relevant estimates can be made. However, it must be kept in mind that estimates are always estimates and therefore cannot claim to be accurate.

Estimates generally take place in the context of Refinement Meetings, which unlike Scrum Events can be held in consultation with the team during the sprint and for which about 10% of the development team's capacity is available. This is i.e. ½ weekday per week.

Although some teams also estimate during the sprint planning meeting, this is less useful because it dilutes the focus of the event and, in the case of questions that arise during the discussion of product backlog items, there is a risk that they cannot be clarified at that time, which means that the product backlog item is either postponed by at least one sprint, or a product backlog item is included in the sprint for which there are still questions, which increases the risk that it cannot be implemented.

It is still possible to include items that are not "Ready" in a Sprint, but this should be the exception.

The most important result is not a number

During a refinement meeting, the focus is often placed on ensuring that as many product backlogs as possible are associated with an estimate at the end of the meeting. Unfortunately this focus is based on a misunderstanding. The main purpose of the Refinement Meeting is to give the roles involved a better understanding of the requirement and to clarify questions that are important for the implementation. This can result in queries to stakeholders, adjustments of requirements or prioritizations, or even in the splitting of product backlog items into smaller packages.

When the requirements are discussed, a central task for the members of the development team is to think along and become familiar with the requirements. This also applies to requirements that are not within their own area of competence. On the one hand, this allows the developers to learn more about other areas, and on the other hand, they contribute with questions or, if necessary, solution approaches from their context to a better understanding of the requirement as a whole and to a better picture of a solution approach together.

Once the questions have been clarified, the team comes to appreciate. Planning Poker based on Story Points has proven to be the best estimation method. There are other estimation parameters, but the mentioned one is superior to the others especially in this context. We will discuss the different methods and their advantages in more detail in the following chapters.

In many teams there are larger discussions based on the estimate, which can generally be summarized under the keyword "Who's right?" and are a waste of time. We are on the level of estimates and who was actually right will only be able to be told after the implementation; until then there are different opinions, nothing more.

But what would be very interesting and important is that the people who made the estimates did so based on an idea of a solution. One person may have identified special risks somewhere, another may have a particularly good solution or components that can be reused. The exchange about these approaches is the actual main benefit of estimates. Based on this exchange, even better ideas may emerge in combination or additional risks or uncertainties may be identified. This may also be the case if all estimators have calculated the same value. It is not about the "price tag", but about the "solution path".

After the exchange, it can be useful for the team to appreciate a second time. The determined value is then used in capacity planning. If there are still deviations in the team, it has proven to be a good idea to agree on a "house rule" in advance, according to which the team will proceed in such a case. This could be, for example, that the team agrees to assign the highest value to the requirement in the 2nd estimate in order to avoid stress in further planning. Other rules are also conceivable. They should also be discussed and adapted in the context of sprint retrospectives if necessary.

It often happens that the same Product Backlog Item is estimated several times during the development process, for example because of changes in the general conditions or additional insights. This is normal and offers the chance to understand requirements even better and to realize even more customer benefits during implementation.

Complexity instead of effort

Again and again one reads about the fact that estimates should not be based on effort, but on "complexity". What is behind this?

If I asked you to give an estimate of the effort required for a certain task, for example mowing a lawn, you would probably briefly consider what tools you have available, how high the lawn is already (could it be that the grass is so high that a normal lawnmower cannot "get through" at all?), what area needs to be mowed and whether there are any other general conditions that might have an influence on the work of mowing the lawn. You would probably tell me a certain duration, which you consider realistic for yourself.

If I were to ask someone else, who, unlike you, has no experience with lawn mowing, and especially would not be able to cope with the motor mower you have included, it is possible that this person would use a completely different, possibly higher value. This would be helped by the fact that he assumed that he was working with a manual lawnmower, and also that he might have included more "buffers" for himself, based on his limited experience.

Who is right now? Whose estimate would be more relevant for the team and its capacity planning? In order to decide this, we would have to define not only what needs to be done but also who will implement a requirement. We would thus definitely be in the context of a group of people, in which everyone carries out their task, and no longer in the context of a team that implements products together.

Accordingly, we try to go another way. We try not to define tasks in dependence on persons, but look for a way to subject the tasks to a general standard, so to speak. We have known this approach for a long time from other subject areas.

If I asked someone how long it would take me to get from Munich to Berlin, they would probably ask me in everyday life how I intend to travel, and depending on whether I fly, travel by train, car or as a hiker, the answer would be different in each case. But my counterpart could also simply tell me the approximate distance of about 500 km and leave it to me to relate this to my kind of travel. It would also make sense to name the order of magnitude instead of an exact number, as this could change depending on the route taken.

This is exactly what we are trying to do when, instead of an implementation effort that would be person-specific, we try to name an abstract order of magnitude "complexity", which - depending on the different competencies of the people involved in the techniques used - can be different.

The fact that different strengths, competencies and speeds occur in a team is already taken into account by specifying the velocity in the planning, so it does not have to be included in the tasks. For sound planning, therefore, it is only necessary that the members of the development team can work largely within the scope of their core competencies. In addition, regular review of planning and estimation and, if necessary, meaningful revision of procedures in the context of continuous improvement is also useful.

Commercial estimates

It happens again and again that organizations use agile estimates in refinements for commercial purposes. Sometimes conversion factors are even defined, according to which a certain financial compensation is due per realized story point. This is not reasonable for several reasons.

Agile estimation, as described, is a basis for planning self-organized teams. It often takes place relatively late, because the team is aware that both requirements and framework conditions change and that more and more is learned about the requirements during the development process. In contrast, commercially relevant effort estimates are usually desired at the beginning of a project or phase, as they become part of a kind of business case and possibly part of offers and contracts. At this point in time, not all requirements are generally clear and there is a relatively large potential for change.

In addition, commercial offers always include aspects such as the question of risk distribution with regard to estimation errors or additional expenses arising in the course of development. When a team is called upon to provide commercial estimates, they will be aware that the estimates are not intended as a basis for planning, but as a firm commitment to a budget. Accordingly, the team will include issues such as risks, deviations, rework and a certain amount of self-protection in such an estimate.

Possibly the team made additionally the experience that with excess of an estimate annoyance threatens, or that the purchase department of the customer withdraws a certain percentage anyway with each estimate. In short, the team will no longer focus on having the best possible planning basis, but will begin to make political prices that are enforceable with the customer, while at the same time ensuring that it offers as little as possible a target for attack.

The result is clear. The estimation will be done with a completely different goal, which leads to the fact that the planning basis for the team and the basis for a continuous improvement of the team processes is undermined by such an approach.

If a team is to provide commercial estimates, it is advisable to keep them separate. Experience has shown that protective mechanisms, in which requirements are sorted into a certain number of orders of magnitude, are usually useful, especially if a lot of information is not yet available when the estimate is performed anyway. Approaches like affinity estimation or groupings based on T-shirt sizes can be useful here.

Story Points, ideal days, working days, t-shirt sizes and dog breeds

The estimation in Scrum and other agile methods is based on very different units in different teams. The most common ones are:

- Story Points
- Ideal days
- Working days
- T-Shirt Sizes
- Dog breeds or similar categorizations

The different units are often associated with specific estimation methods or specific targets.

Story Points are a virtual unit as already shown. In addition to focusing on complexity instead of effort, they have the advantage that they are clearly not time units such as days, hours or the like. Thus, people will (at least in theory) be less likely to succumb to the misunderstanding of converting corresponding estimates into calendar days or the like. This has several advantages. First, it reduces the risk of blaming according to the pattern "You have estimated 3 days and now it's day 5 and you're still not finished" (although even with effort estimates in days, it is not the time from start to finish that is estimated, but the time that is estimated to reduce a task, which can vary considerably due to queries, waiting times, etc.).

In addition, the fact that estimates are not made in units of time can emphasize the fact that it is not a matter of effort estimates, but rather of a measure of complexity and that different people will have different efforts for this.

Story Points are generally estimated in even numbers. The use of a series of numbers derived [6]from the Fibonacci sequence of numbers

---

[6] Wikipedia.de writes about it:

"The Fibonacci sequence is the infinite sequence of natural numbers, which (originally) begins with twice the number 1 or (often, in modern notation) is additionally provided with a leading number 0. In the following, the sum of two successive numbers results in the number immediately following:

has proven to be a good solution. In most cases, the number sequence is slightly modified and looks like this:

0,1,2,3,5,8,13,20,40,100

What is important is not the origin or original statement. It is more important, that I have a series of numbers, which has very small distances in the lower part, but more and more to the top. Alternatively, some teams also use a series of numbers, which corresponds to the powers of two 2^0, 2^1, 2^2, ...

The reason behind this is that although it is possible to distinguish in estimates whether something is about twice or three times as big as something else, a discussion about whether something is 40 or 41

0, 1, 1, 2, 3, 5, 8, 13, 21, 34, 55 ...

The numbers contained in it are called Fibonacci numbers. The sequence is named after Leonardo Fibonacci, who described the growth of a rabbit population in 1202. The sequence was already known in ancient times to both the Greeks and the Indians.

Further research showed that the Fibonacci sequence also describes numerous other growth processes in nature. It appears to be a kind of growth pattern in nature".

times as big as something else is rather pointless - at least as long as one is within the range of the estimate.

A central step is only the question to which task the value "1" is assigned. This is often referred to as the reference story. The selection is relatively simple. It should be a relatively less complex task whose requirements are comprehensible for the members of the team. All other product items are then expressed in relation to it.

Ideal days - *ideal hours*

Ideal day estimation is about teams wanting to emphasize that the estimation is not about working days or calendar days, but about how much work would be involved if a task could be performed full-time. Tasks that employees perform in addition, such as answering e-mails, possibly telephone calls, meetings, etc., are therefore not included. In many teams that work in this way, there are fixed conversion rates, such as 1 working day corresponds to 6 ideal hours; accordingly, a task that was estimated to take place on 5 ideal days (5x8 ideal hours), for example, would make up 40 ideal hours, which in turn would correspond to slightly less than 7 working days.

Working days

Like ideal days, working days are always based on effort and not on complexity. In practice, this often leads to big discussions, because the effort can vary greatly depending on the person who implements a requirement. Some teams have corresponding conversion agreements, according to which, for example, a less experienced colleague always multiplies his estimates by X or similar. Personally, I do not consider ideal days or working days to be sensible. Their deployment often has to do with teams resisting the deployment of a "new" Story Points unit. In action, both measures are rather disadvantageous.

T-Shirt Sizes

T-shirt sizes are used by teams to classify product backlog items into a few categories. S, M, L, XL are usually the categories used. This can be very helpful to get a rough overview of requirements. Especially in the context of an early rough estimation - e.g. to assign requirements to individual releases or to create commercial offers - such categorizations can be helpful. With regard to sprint planning, on the other hand, the form of categorization is often too unspecific and imprecise, which accordingly reduces sprint planning and the possibility of optimizing it.

Dog breeds and similar categorizations

Some teams have their own ways of categorizing requirements and thus more precisely determining the implementation effort. Some of them are very imaginative, like a team I met that categorized its product backlog items by dog breed. Without reproducing the whole conversion table, I remembered that one Product Backlog Item, which the team had estimated with "Great Dane", caused the same amount of effort as sixteen Backlog Items estimated with "Chihuahua". Basically, this is a variant of the estimation based on T-shirt sizes.

Incorrect estimates as a success factor - why we should make more mistakes

Actually, it is not so much about making more mistakes or misjudging. Of course it is ideal if we don't make any mistakes and the estimates we make as a team correspond to reality. This enables us to plan in the best possible way.

However, errors (also with regard to estimates) are quasi normal. It is about estimates, where deviations are part of the procedure. Teams which do not detect any deviations and whose estimates and plans simply "fit" are very often teams which do not focus on continuous improvement and therefore do not estimate ambitiously, but rather design estimates and plans in such a way that they no longer pose a challenge, but can be realized in any case.

Making mistakes is part of agility. Whether it is in the context of estimation or in the context of other measures. Teams that do not make mistakes are generally often teams that focus too little on the aspect of continuous improvement and therefore do not look for ways to become better.

Estimate tasks?

In the course of the Sprint Planning Meeting, the first step is to define what is to be implemented in the next Sprint. In the second part of the meeting, the development team will mainly deal with the question of which work packages (tasks) they need to implement the selected product backlog items.

Some teams decide to estimate the tasks individually at first. Ideal hours or working hours are often chosen as units of measurement. This can help teams to further objectify their estimates and see during the sprint whether the assumptions made can be implemented. This should enable early reaction in case of deviations.

In fact, this approach creates a certain amount of additional feeling of security, although in many cases this is very deceptive. We are in the realm of estimates. Efforts are estimated, capacities are estimated - if details are estimated now, it only means that instead of two different estimates, we compare three and try to draw conclusions based on them. Even the loss of an employee due to illness, accident or the like, or the fact that a team member may have to support a colleague outside the team without planning, or that a required resource may not be available at the moment, can lead to the collapse of the whole beautiful detailed planning.

For a reasonable planning and to get an overview of the sprint progress it is generally sufficient to ensure that work packages of one to two days maximum are available. This also allows you to determine if implementations are delayed and the planning effort remains clear. In this context, it is also sufficient, in my experience, if the monitoring is based on the number of work packages in Sprint Burndown Charts.

Estimation methods

In the course of the last years different estimation methods have developed, which are used by different agile methods in different contexts. Some of those, which are also used in the context of Scrum, will be described in more detail here:

- Planning Poker
- Triangulation
- T-Shirt Sizes
- Bucket System (The Bucket System)
- Large / uncertain / small (Big / Uncertain / Small)

Planning Poker

The procedure in connection with Planning Poker has already been described in previous chapters. Planning Poker is mainly used as a basis for sprint planning within the Refinement.

Triangulation

Triangulation is not an own method, but an extension of Planning Poker. Unlike traditional Planning Poker, which generally works with one reference story, Triangulation works with two reference stories of different length and complexity. Thus, by relating a product backlog item with two different reference stories, it is possible to estimate more accurately. It is not necessary that one of the stories corresponds to the reference value "1". It would also be conceivable to perform a triangulation with one story with value "5" and one with value "40" in order to better evaluate even more extensive stories. The statement about the story to be estimated would be: Story "X" is half as large as the reference story with value "40" and about 5 times as large as the story with reference value "5".

This procedure does not necessarily have to be implemented permanently. In many teams it corresponds to the normal, intuitive procedure in which newly estimated stories are compared with already known stories from previous sprints that have already been implemented or other stories that have already been estimated.

T-Shirt Sizes

Estimates in T-shirt sizes are usually made at a time when we don't know too much about the individual requirements and many questions are still open. So it is generally a matter of a rough sorting of requirements and not of a detailed estimation of effort. When we apply this estimation method, we generally realize that the results are subject to a wider range, but especially in cases where an overview is required, this is usually in a range that is nevertheless useful because it gives us an understanding of orders of magnitude.

The procedure is relatively simple. Different areas are defined, which are named after the different t-shirt sizes. Possibly "S" is defined as an effort of 1-3 days, "M" as 3-5 days or similar. The individual stories are now assigned to the respective columns by the team together. This can be done either through discussions or through other agile estimation methods as described below.

T-shirt-size approaches are also very well suited for making commercial estimates for the preparation of offers. The idea that these are approximate estimates and not binding expenditure figures is already apparent from the fact that the estimate refers to certain ranges of tension.

Bucket system

The "bucket system" is a way to estimate a large number of elements with a small to medium group of people and to do this quickly.

The bucket estimation system works as follows:

1. Make sure that all the elements to be estimated are written on cards and draw a numbered line on the table or on the wall, arranging the different buckets of the desired size according to their size. These can be physical buckets, or areas to which cards will later be assigned. Many teams use a

sequence of numbers for this, which corresponds to the Fibonacci sequence.

2. Select a random item from the collection. Read it to the group. Put it in the bucket "8". This article is our first reference article.

3. Randomly select another item from the collection. Read it to the group. The group discusses its relative position on the scale. Once consensus is reached, place the article in the appropriate bucket. Note: The estimate is only to be seen in relation to the article already placed in the bucket. This has no relation to the Story Points you might use otherwise.

4. Choose a third point at random and place it in the appropriate bucket after discussion and consensus has been reached.

5. If the random elements have moved the scale significantly towards one end or the other, rescale the elements (e.g. if the first element is actually very small and should be in bucket "1").

6. Assign all remaining items equally to all participants. Each participant places items on the scale without discussion with other participants. If a person has an item that they really don't understand, that item can be offered to another person.

7. Everyone quietly checks the elements on the scale. If a participant finds an element that he or she feels is not in the right place, he or she is welcome to point it out to the group. The group then discusses until a consensus is reached and the element is placed in one of the buckets.

8. Write the bucket numbers on the cards to record the estimates.

Some important points should be noted:

- Several articles can be in the same bucket.
- Elements must always be assigned to a bucket. There must be none between the buckets.
- If the scale has to be shifted, the participants should also discuss whether this might result in changed distances between the shifted elements (e.g. because the scale distances have now become larger).
- Everyone must participate in the distribution.
- Discussions always take place within the entire team and not between individuals.
- During the distribution, when the individual participants assign entries, no discussion is held. This happens in silence.

Large/unsure/small

A very fast method for rough estimation is the large/unsure/small method. The team is asked to classify the items into one of these categories. The first step is to divide the obvious items into the two extreme categories. Next, the group can discuss the more complex elements. This is actually a simplification of the bucket system. The system is particularly suitable for smaller groups with similar items. Next, you can assign sizes to these 3 categories.

Bibliography

- Cohn, Mike. Agile Softwareentwicklung: Mit Scrum Zum Erfolg! Addison-Wesley, 2010.

- Cohn, Mike. *Agile Estimating and Planning*. Prentice Hall PTR, 2012.

- MULLER, PAUL C. *AGILE LEADERSHIP IM SCRUM-KONTEXT: Servant Leadership Für Agile Leader Und Solche, Die Es... Werden Wollen*. BOOKS ON DEMAND, 2020.

- Marfurt, Markus. *Taschen-Guide Zur Professional Scrum Master-Zertifizierung (PSM 1)*. Epubli, 2017.

- Ries, Eric, and Ursula Bischoff. *Lean Startup: Schnell, Risikolos Und Erfolgreich Unternehmen gründen*. Redline-Verl., 2017.

- Sutherland, Jeff. *Das Scrum Praxisbuch*. Campus Verlag, 2020.

- Sutherland, Jeff. *Scrum: the Art of Doing Twice the Work in Half the Time*. Business News Publishing, 2016.